T0052740

Since 1888, *National Geographic* magazine has provided its readers a wealth of information and helped us understand the world in which we live. Insightful articles, supported by gorgeous photography and impeccable research, bring the mission of the National Geographic Society front and center: to inspire people to care about the planet. The *Explore* series delivers *National Geographic* to you in the same spirit. Each of the books in this series presents the best articles on popular and relevant topics in an accessible format. In addition, each book highlights the work of National Geographic Explorers, photographers, and writers. Explore the world of *National Geographic*. You will be inspired.

ON THE COVER
Violent dust storm approaching downtown Phoenix, Arizona

Over the past century, it has gotten easier to ignore the weather. More and more people around the world have central heat in the winter and air conditioning in the summer. Good roads, four-wheel drive vehicles, cell phones, and GPS systems make travel possible even in storms that would have paralyzed earlier travelers.

But there are still times when the elements demand our attention. Earthquakes and giant waves kill hundreds of thousands. Floods, droughts, and tornadoes cause billions of dollars worth of damage. In recent decades, disasters due to natural causes have become more costly—in both money and lives. One reason for this is that people are building ever more homes in areas that are at risk when the strongest storms or waves hit. Many scientists also believe that global warming is making the situation worse.

Now more than ever, understanding extreme weather is key to minimizing damage and loss of life. We are not totally helpless against the forces of nature. More accurate forecasting and more thoughtful choices about where we build can help save the lives and property of people you know—maybe even yours.

Many of the articles in this book, adapted from National Geographic publications, tell of scientists making new discoveries about extreme weather. One of these scientists, National Geographic Explorer Tim Samaras, gave his life in the pursuit of knowledge about how tornadoes work. In 2013, Samaras, his son Paul, and his research partner Carl Young were killed when their car took a direct hit from a massive tornado they were tracking. Tim was not following the tornado for the thrill of it. He believed that discovering more about tornadoes would help engineers design early warning systems that could save many lives. This book is dedicated to the memory of Tim Samaras, a National Geographic Explorer, distinguished scientist, and friend.

IN MEMORIAM: TIM SAMARAS
Tim Samaras did not just chase storms. He pursued knowledge that could save the lives of thousands.

EPIC STORMS

Adapted from "Epic Storms," by Jeremy Berlin,
in *National Geographic*, July 2012

TAIL END
A dying tornado like this one in
Regan, North Dakota, is said to
be in the "roping out" phase.

In shockingly clear black-and-white, photographer Mitch Dobrowner captures amazing moments in the lives of epic storms.

MIGHTY DISPLAYS

"Some things you learn best in calm," wrote author Willa Cather, scribe of the Great Plains, "and some in storm." She wasn't talking about the local weather, but she might as well have been. Each year the American western plains offer an advanced class in natural uproar. From March to October the prairie plays host to thousands of visible, violent storms. Weather and topography (or the shape of the land) work together to put on blustery and mighty displays.

It starts when dry air from the Rockies slides over moist air from the Gulf of Mexico. The stage is set for a storm that may bring rain, hail, lightning, high winds—even a tornado. It may kill people and animals, destroy crops and property, and flood roads and towns.

The National Weather Service reports dozens of storm-related deaths every year. In 2011, says the insurance industry, thunderstorms in the United States were to blame for $26 billion in damage. Yet storms also deliver welcome rain to dry fields.

STORM IN THE DESERT
Resembling a mushroom cloud, a massive thunderstorm drops a drenching rain on the desert near Lordsburg, New Mexico. The base of this cloud may hang some two miles above the ground.

OMINOUS SKIES
(left) A hailstorm breaches the hills near Moorcroft, Wyoming. (right) This storm over Guymon, Oklahoma, bristles with electricity. "No two storms are the same," says James LaDue, a meteorologist at the National Weather Service. "No two skies are either."

They also drive power-generating windmills. Even lightning contributes by adding nitrogen to the soil.

SUPERCELLS AND SQUALLS

Mitch Dobrowner, a landscape photographer, is used to shooting things that don't move. So in order to record these remarkable storms, he was helped by famous storm chaser Roger Hill, a witness to more than 600 tornadoes.

Over the past three years, they have used mobile satellite data and radar imaging to chase some 45 weather systems over 16 states. They sometimes drive 900 miles in a day to capture a moment, and the results are amazing. "With storms," says Dobrowner, "it's like shooting a sporting event. Things happen so quickly, I really have to adapt." Working in black and white—"Color seems too everyday," he says—Dobrowner purposely seeks out storms called **supercells**, the mightiest of all the thunderstorms.

A supercell, says Hill, "is the most violent, **prolific** tornado-producing machine there is." These storms require moist, unstable air, something to lift the air, and vertical **wind shear** to rotate the storm.

When those elements align, the results can be unpredictable. Powered by a strong, rotating column of rising air, a supercell can steer itself in any direction. It can destroy other **squalls** in its path. It can dodge its own storm-extinguishing

No two skies are either." —JAMES LADUE

precipitation, staying alive for up to 12 hours as it barges over the landscape.

Indeed, both Dobrowner and Hill see supercells as living things. Born under the right conditions, they can gain strength as they grow, changing shape, fighting for life, eventually dying. Describing the storms in this way does not remove the danger. In the wild West, says Hill, storms demand respect. "I feel honored to be shooting them," says Dobrowner.

THINK ABOUT IT! ||||||||||||||||||||||||||||||||||||

1 Make Generalizations Why is it necessary to learn more about supercells and tornadoes?

2 Compare and Contrast What are the positive and negative aspects of thunderstorms?

3 Analyze Visuals Choose one photo from the article. How does the photo help support the photographer's impression that big storms are living things?

BACKGROUND & VOCABULARY

precipitation *n.* (prih-sih-puh-TAY-shuhn) the moisture that falls as rain, snow, sleet, or hail

prolific *adj.* (proh-LIH-fihk) producing a large number

squall *n.* (skwal) a sudden gust of wind that often occurs with thunderstorms

supercell *n.* (SOO-pur-sehl) a thunderstorm with a constantly rotating column of rising air

wind shear *n.* a change in the speed or direction of wind within a short distance

WEATH

Gone Wild

Adapted from "Weather Gone Wild," by Peter Miller,
in *National Geographic*, September 2012

CUMBERLAND OVERFLOW
In May of 2010, flooding in
Nashville, Tennessee, caused the
Cumberland River to overflow,
submerging the neighborhood of
Pennington Bend.

Across the globe, the weather has been setting records, but nobody's applauding. Tornadoes, floods, droughts, and hurricanes have affected the lives of millions. Find out what may be causing recent extremes of weather.

A FLOOD IN NASHVILLE

The weekend forecast for Nashville, Tennessee, called for two to four inches of rain. But by the afternoon of Saturday, May 1, 2010, six inches had fallen in some places, and it was still raining.

Mayor Karl Dean was in the city's "war room" watching reports of flooding when he saw something shocking on the television screens. The Cumberland River was overflowing into Interstate 24. A 40-foot-long steel building floated past cars caught in the flood.

"We've got a building running into cars," said the anchorman.

When Mayor Dean saw the floating building, he realized how extreme the situation had become. Rescue teams were sent out in boats. One team plucked the driver of a truck from chest-high water. Others pulled families off rooftops. Still, 11 people died in the city that weekend.

Nashville had never seen a storm like this. At a local television station, meteorologist Charlie Neese could see that the **jet stream** was stuck over the city. One thunderstorm after another was sucking up humid air from the Gulf of Mexico and dumping the water on Nashville. While Neese was broadcasting from a second-floor studio, the first-floor newsroom was flooded by backed-up sewers.

The Cumberland River, which runs through Nashville, started rising Saturday morning. At Ingram Barge Company, David Edgin had more than 77 boats and barges on the river. He called the U.S. Army Corps of Engineers to ask how high the river would rise. "We've never seen anything like this," they said. Edgin ordered his boats to find safe locations along the riverbank. It turned out to be a smart move.

By Saturday night the Cumberland had risen to 35 feet, but the rain continued until Monday. The river crested at 52 feet, 12 feet above flood stage. The flood spilled into downtown streets, causing two billion dollars in damage. Some parts of Nashville had seen more than 13 inches of rain—about twice the previous record.

CHANGING PATTERNS

There's been a change in the weather. Extreme events like the Nashville flood are happening more often. A month before the Nashville disaster, torrential downpours in Rio de Janeiro, Brazil, triggered mud slides that buried hundreds. In late 2011 floods in Thailand submerged hundreds of factories, creating a worldwide shortage of computer hard drives.

And it's not just rain making headlines. Severe droughts have occurred in Texas, Australia, Russia, and East Africa. Deadly heat waves have hit Europe, and tornadoes have ripped across the United States. In 2011, weather disasters cost about $150 billion worldwide, 25 percent more than the year before.

What's going on? Are these extreme events signals of a human-made change in Earth's climate? Or is it just a natural stretch of bad luck?

The short answer is: probably both. The main forces behind recent disasters have been natural climate cycles like **El Niño** and **La Niña**. During El Niño events, warm water normally found in the central Pacific moves east to South America; during La Niña events, it retreats into the western Pacific. As the warm water moves back and forth along the Equator, the jet stream moves north and south, changing the tracks that storms follow. El Niño pushes rain storms over the southern United States while bringing drought to Australia. La Niña floods Australia with rain and brings drought to the American Southwest. Thus, extreme El Niño or La Niña events cause extreme weather elsewhere.

But natural cycles don't explain everything. Something else is happening: Earth is getting warmer, and there is more moisture in the air. The buildup of **greenhouse gases** in the atmosphere is trapping heat and warming up the planet. The average surface temperature worldwide has risen nearly one degree Fahrenheit in 40 years. In 2010 it reached a record 58.12°F.

As the oceans warm, they give off more water vapor. Over the past 25 years water vapor in the air has increased by four percent. The more water vapor, the greater chance of heavy rainfall. By the end of the century the average world temperature could rise as much as eight degrees Fahrenheit.

The greatest changes have occurred in the Arctic Ocean, which has lost 40 percent of its summer sea ice since the 1980s. Autumn temperatures have risen, as dark waters absorb sunlight that ice once reflected back into space. Warming is also changing the path of the polar jet stream around the planet—which might explain why North America was so warm in the winter of 2011 and Europe was so cold. Wandering farther north into Canada, the jet stream brought unusually warm air. Dipping farther south into Europe, it brought more cold and snow. The next year, eastern North America got the heavy snow. Since the jet stream moves around every year, extreme weather may too.

When it comes to individual storms, scientists don't know what effect global warming might have. Extra water vapor in the atmosphere might cause more big storms such as hurricanes. Some models predict that global warming could increase the average strength of hurricanes, but it isn't clear if that has happened yet. And the same models that predict bigger hurricanes also predict that fewer will occur.

The tornado data is even more unclear. A hotter, wetter atmosphere should cause more thunderstorms, but it might also reduce the **wind shear** needed to form twisters. More tornadoes reported in the United States might simply mean that more people are looking for them. The number of severe tornadoes may not be increasing at all. The spring of 2011 was one of the worst tornado seasons in United States history, but scientists don't yet know if global warming was to blame.

In the case of some weather extremes, though, there is no doubt about the cause. The warmer atmosphere clearly causes more record-breaking heat waves. Rainfall has increased along with moisture in the atmosphere. The amount of rain falling in the heaviest downpours has increased

DOWNSTAIRS DOWNPOUR
In Chengdu, China, rainwater cascades down a flight of stairs from an underground garage. The 2011 downpour flooded streets and knocked out electricity.

by nearly 20 percent in the past century in the United States. "You're getting more rain from a given storm now than you would have 30 or 40 years ago," says Gerald Meehl, a senior scientist at the National Center for Atmospheric Research in Boulder, Colorado.

DROUGHT TAKES HOLD

While some places like Nashville have gotten too much rain, others haven't gotten enough. The residents of the West Texas town of Robert Lee spent much of 2011 watching their water supply dry up. The local reservoir—an artificial or natural lake used for water supply—lost more than 99 percent of its water. In January 2012 the town began building a pipeline to Bronte, a town with wells, not just a reservoir.

Less rain fell on Texas from October 2010 to September 2011 than in any other 12-month period since record keeping began. The whole state suffered, but West Texas suffered the most. All across the region farmers, ranchers, and towns felt the damage.

The drought withered grazing lands too, forcing ranchers to ship livestock to greener pastures up north. The Four Sixes Ranch near Guthrie drove more than 4,000 head of cattle onto trucks headed to lands leased in Nebraska and Montana. The last time they attempted such a thing was more than a century ago, when the ranch moved herds to Oklahoma. This drought was worse. By July the ranch had run out of tank water—drinking water in dirt ponds for cattle.

ICEBOUND
Frozen spray from Lake Geneva, in Switzerland, buries cars and trees in 2012. An unusual dip in the polar jet stream brought Arctic air and deep snows to Europe.

"This has been the most severe one-year drought we've ever had," said Texas **climatologist** John Nielsen-Gammon. On top of that, Texans sweated through the hottest summer in memory in 2011. Dallas saw the mercury climb to 100°F or higher on 71 days.

There's no mystery about the main cause of the drought, Nielsen-Gammon said: It was La Niña, which pushed storm tracks farther north over the United States, reducing rainfall throughout the South. "We just happened to be right in the center of it," he said.

But global warming made a bad heat wave even worse. "Under normal conditions a lot of the sun's energy gets used to evaporate water from the soil or from plants," Nielsen-Gammon explained. "But when there's no water to evaporate, all that energy goes into heating the

ground and the air. Given how little rain we had, we probably would have had record warmth in Texas in 2011 even without climate change. But climate change added an additional degree or so of heat to it," he continued.

That extra degree of heat made the state's forests more likely to burn. More heat means more water evaporates from the land, leaving forests drier. In 2011, Texas had its worst wildfire season ever. One of the costliest fires started in a state park near Austin, where pine trees were extremely dry. Fanned by strong winds, the blaze raced south through suburban neighborhoods and burned 1,685 houses.

The rising cost of natural disasters can be blamed only partly on the weather. The increase in damage is also due to more people living in vulnerable areas. In Southwestern states

> *"To put it bluntly, we're doing a lousy job keeping up with disasters."*
> — MICHAEL OPPENHEIMER

many new neighborhoods are being built near woodlands, exposed to wildfires. In the Southeast expensive beach houses and hotels are exposed to hurricanes and other storms.

"Something has gone wrong," says Michael Oppenheimer, a climatologist at Princeton University. "To put it bluntly, we're doing a lousy job keeping up with disasters."

COPING WITH NEW REALITIES

Insurance companies are suffering consequences. Insured losses from natural disasters in the United States in 2011 totaled nearly $36 billion, 50 percent higher than the previous decade.

In Florida, where hurricanes, wildfires, and drought pose huge risks to insurers, several firms have stopped writing new policies. They can't afford another disaster like Hurricane Andrew, which cost the industry an estimated $25 billion in 1992. To fill the gap, the state government created the Citizens Property Insurance Corporation, which has become Florida's largest provider of homeowner's insurance. But the new system may not have the resources to survive a big storm.

Meanwhile other countries are trying to prepare better for extreme weather. An exceptional heat wave in Europe in 2003 took 35,000 lives, and one study found that climate change had doubled the chances of such a disaster. Afterward French cities set up air-conditioned shelters and identified people who would need transportation to the

shelters. When another heat wave hit in 2006, the death rate was two-thirds lower.

A tropical storm killed some 500,000 people in Bangladesh in 1970. Afterward the government began an early warning system and built shelters for evacuated families. Today, storm death counts are much lower.

Better responses to weather disasters help, but can anything be done to make them less likely? The best approach to extreme weather is to attack all the risk factors. Some examples: planting crops that resist drought, building houses that resist floods, discouraging people from building in dangerous places, and finding ways to release less greenhouse gas into the atmosphere.

We need to face that reality, Oppenheimer believes, and do the things we know can save lives and money. Says Oppenheimer, "We don't have to just stand there and take it."

THINK ABOUT IT!

1 **Analyze Cause and Effect** Which types of disaster are most closely linked to global warming?

2 **Evaluate** What actions would be most effective in reducing future storm damage in Florida and along the southeastern coast?

3 **Compare and Contrast** What are the main differences between El Niño and La Niña?

BACKGROUND & VOCABULARY

climatologist *n.* (kly-muh-TAWL-uh-jihst) a scientist who studies weather patterns over long periods of time

El Niño *n.* (ehl NEE-nyoh) a pool of warm Pacific Ocean water that flows east along the equator during December

greenhouse gases *n.* the gases in the atmosphere that trap heat and contribute to global warming

jet stream *n.* a long narrow current of fast-flowing winds high above Earth's surface that blow from the west

La Niña *n.* (la NEE-nyah) a pool of cool Pacific Ocean water that rises to the surface when warmer water is pushed to the west

wind shear *n.* a change in the speed or direction of wind within a short distance

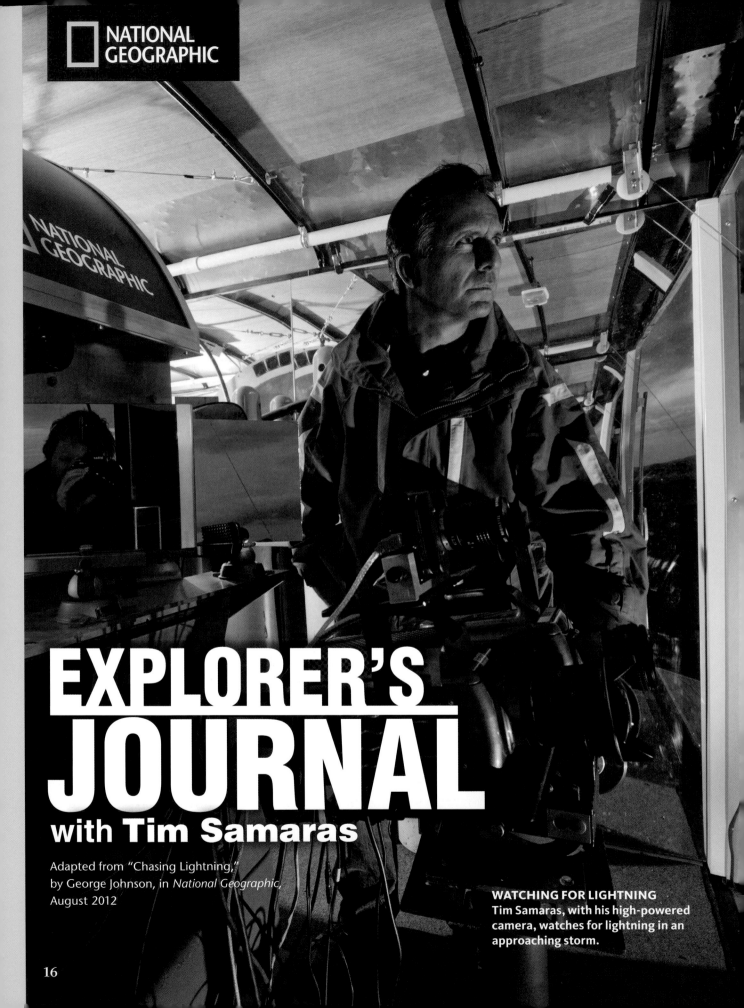

NATIONAL GEOGRAPHIC

EXPLORER'S
JOURNAL
with **Tim Samaras**

Adapted from "Chasing Lightning,"
by George Johnson, in *National Geographic*,
August 2012

WATCHING FOR LIGHTNING
Tim Samaras, with his high-powered
camera, watches for lightning in an
approaching storm.

How do you capture lightning and get it to give up its secrets? National Geographic Explorer Tim Samaras was determined to learn all about why lightning behaves as it does.

Tim Samaras was killed on May 31, 2013, by a tornado he was following. He was pursuing knowledge about these deadly storms, hoping to someday develop a way to accurately warn people who might be in a tornado's path. In 2012, writer George Johnson joined Samaras on his quest to understand another weather mystery: lightning.

ONE EYE ON THE ROAD

Luckily, there's a **rumble strip** running along the shoulder of the highway, because Tim Samaras can't keep his eyes on the road. It's summer, and he's driving a big pickup truck pulling a 16-foot trailer outfitted with high-speed cameras and other gear. A laptop mounted to his right, Samaras has one hand on the steering wheel and the other on the computer's trackball. He is mousing his way around a weather radar map of the Oklahoma Panhandle. A blob of colors—red in the middle, surrounded by orange, yellow, green, and blue—shows a thunderstorm forming northeast of Boise City.

"It's starting to spit out some pretty good lightning," he says, glancing again at the radar on the screen of his laptop. Then comes the buzzing of his tires against the rumble strip, and he calmly steers the rolling laboratory back onto the road.

We pass through Boise City, following the storm east. Clouds are boiling up like cauliflower, the classic sign of the warm, moist **updrafts** that cause lightning. No one knows exactly why, but rising air separates negatively charged water droplets and ice particles from positive ones. The result is a multimillion-volt flash in the sky.

"Did you just see that strike?" Samaras exclaims. He looks at the radar, and then back at the road. "See how that storm is anchored right there? That's what we want."

The flashes are coming every few seconds now, and the tires keep hitting the rumble strip. But just as he's looking for a place to pull over, the blob on the radar starts shrinking. Samaras picks up speed, but it's too late—soon the sun has reappeared and a rainbow is arcing overhead.

"Whenever you see the rainbow, it's game over," he says. But at 6 p.m. his day is just beginning. The radar shows a storm forming over southern Kansas, 80 miles away.

TO CATCH A LIGHTNING BOLT

Every thunderstorm season since 2006 Samaras has been trying to do the impossible: photograph a lightning strike the moment it is born. A strike typically begins with a descending zigzag of negatively charged electricity, called a stepped leader. When it gets near enough to the ground, positive fingers of charge reach up from the earth. Then they come together in a dazzling 30,000 **amp** surge of current. Traveling at a third of the speed of light, it leaps toward the sky. The burst of light from this "return stroke" is what we see. The entire process takes as little as 200 milliseconds.

Samaras has two Phantoms, high-speed cameras that shoot 10,000 frames per second. They allow him to capture stunning slow-motion videos of downward stepped leaders and occasionally of upward streamers. But as soon as the two connect—an event called the attachment process—the flash from the return stroke blinds the camera.

Lying within the perfect photo might be clues to some of lightning's mysteries. Why does lightning sometimes strike a low tree when there's a taller metal tower nearby? Why does lightning strike at all? The voltages produced in thunderclouds are strong, but not nearly enough

to overcome the **insulating** properties of air. A photo of the attachment process might suggest an answer. Getting the photo is impossible without a camera capable of shooting more than a million frames per second. There's only one such camera, and it's in Samaras's trailer.

Weighing 1,600 pounds, the camera was developed to photograph nuclear tests during the Cold War. The massive instrument is a marvel of technology from before the digital age. Light entering its main lens strikes a three-sided mirror, which sits at the center of a **turbine**. Rotating as fast as 6,000 revolutions per second, the mirror sweeps the light across the lenses of 35-millimeter film cameras mounted around the rim. The result is a sequence of images less than one-millionth of a second apart. Samaras calls the weighty camera the Kahuna.

With funding assistance from National Geographic, he installed digital sensors designed for deep space and added custom software and circuitry. But no matter what you do, an instrument weighing almost a ton is hard to move into position. For each shot you have to wait about ten seconds for the turbine to spin up to speed. It takes 20 minutes to download the data to see what you've got. Only then can you try another shot. In other words, Samaras needs a storm that's not moving, right where the camera is pointing. And although some research facilities can produce manufactured lightning by firing rockets into storm clouds, Samaras is only interested in the natural kind.

He is used to people telling him what can't be done. Before he started following lightning, he spent several years chasing tornadoes. He designed electronic probes to lie in the likely path of a tornado. They had video cameras and instruments to take various readings. People were doubtful about that too, but he managed to gather some of the most accurate tornado data ever recorded.

Hoping to catch up to the storm, we head north, where a dark mass of clouds is building

18

over the plains. As the sun sets, the tops of the clouds cool, which means more lightning. By the time we pull to the side of the road, the storm is so violent that it has spun off a small tornado. The twister quickly disappears, leaving a spectacular lightning show. In the trailer, a wall of video screens displays weather information and an electronic voice announces the distance of the strikes: "17 miles, 15 miles, 11 miles." Then: "Very high electric field."

"The electric-field meter is going absolutely nuts," Samaras observes. A sensor shows that the charge of the atmosphere is high and rising, meaning it's dangerous outside. The two Phantoms capture images before and during the lightning flashes, but the conditions just aren't right for getting a shot with the Kahuna.

MAKING LIGHTNING

By the time I saw Samaras again, two years later, he had reluctantly decided to try aiming his camera at rocket-triggered lightning at Langmuir's Laboratory for Atmospheric Research in Socorro, New Mexico.

Built in 1963, the laboratory sits in the path of moisture that flows up each summer from the south. Sheltered inside an underground bunker called the Kiva, a researcher remotely fires rockets, each connected to a long wire, into a highly charged storm cloud. Colleagues at another location record the strike with a Phantom and other instruments.

Bill Winn, head of the lab, greeted Samaras.

"You should have been here today," Winn said. "We had three strikes."

"Figures," Samaras said.

One of the scientists explained that at the right time a rocket would be armed and a five-second countdown would begin. Samaras looked worried.

Since the Kahuna took ten seconds to spin up to speed, he would have to idle the turbine at a slow pace to keep it from overheating, then crank it up before the countdown began.

Samaras waited patiently, and a promising storm arrived on the third day. By late afternoon the rain was heavy, turning briefly to hail. We watched lightning from inside the trailer—then the radio call: "Kiva is arming rockets."

I huddled on the trailer floor, shifting my attention between the weather outside and the radar on the laptop. Wind was rocking us back and forth. Then the Kiva requested a **launch window**, and Samaras began idling the turbine. The countdown began and Samaras ramped up the speed. In the sky above us a rocket fired, and its long, trailing wire was vaporized by lightning. But it happened too quickly. As Samaras had feared, the five-second window was too narrow. Over the next hour the Kiva triggered three strikes, but the Kahuna could not be readied in time. Samaras left the mountain with some beautiful imagery from the Phantoms but without the Kahuna shot.

Samaras was far from giving up the chase.

"I'm still in hot pursuit of that image," he told me. "And I won't stop until this is done."

THINK ABOUT IT! ||||||||||||||||||||||||||||||||

1 Identify Problems and Solutions What were the limitations of taking photos with the Kahuna, and what was Tim Samaras doing to overcome them?

2 Form and Support Opinions Do you think photographing lightning is worth the effort and expense Samaras put into it? Why or why not?

BACKGROUND & VOCABULARY

amp *n.* an abbreviation for *ampere* (AM-peer), a unit of measurement for electric current

insulating *adj.* (IN-suh-lay-ting) here, preventing the flow of electricity

launch window *n.* a short span of time during which an event can begin

rumble strip *n.* a rough strip of pavement near the edge of a roadway that alerts a driver to return to the lane

turbine *n.* (TUR-bihn) a type of engine that converts a flow of air or water into a spinning motion

updraft *n.* an upward movement of air

The CALM Before the WAVE

Adapted from "The Calm Before the Wave,"
by Tim Folger, in *National Geographic*, February 2012

CALM FOR NOW
Heceta Head Light House watches
over coastal waters of the Pacific
Ocean near Florence, Oregon.

GIANT WAVES CALLED TSUNAMIS, WHICH ARE CAUSED BY UNDERSEA EARTHQUAKES, CAN CAUSE MASSIVE DEVASTATION. SCIENTISTS ARE STUDYING TSUNAMIS AND SEARCHING FOR WAYS TO WARN COASTAL DWELLERS IN TIME TO FLEE WHEN ONE OF THESE DEADLY WAVES HEADS FOR LAND.

SWEPT AWAY

Jin Sato is the mayor of a town that no longer exists. Minamisanriku, a quiet fishing port in northeastern Japan, disappeared on March 11, 2011. Sato nearly did too. The disaster started about 80 miles east in the Pacific Ocean, along a **fault** deep beneath the seafloor. A 280-mile-long block of Earth's crust suddenly lurched to the east. Sato had just attended a meeting at the town hall. "We were talking about the town's tsunami defenses," he says. Another earthquake had jolted the region two days before the March 11 quake, the largest in Japan's history.

When the ground finally stopped moving, Minamisanriku was still mostly intact. Sato and several co-workers ran to the town's three-story disaster-readiness center. On the second floor, Miki Endo started broadcasting a warning over the town's loudspeakers: "Please head to higher ground!" Sato and others headed for the roof and watched the tsunami pour over the town's 18-foot-high seawall, sweeping away everything in its path. Then dark gray water surged over the top of their building. Endo's broadcasts stopped.

Some 16,000 people died that day, most of whom lived along the coasts in Japan's Tohoku region. The tsunami destroyed towns and left hundreds of thousands homeless. Those lost in Minamisanriku included Miki Endo. Sato only survived by clinging to a radio antenna on the roof. "I think I was underwater for three or four minutes," he says. "It's hard to say." Many of the 30 or so people on the roof tried to hang onto iron railings as the wave repeatedly washed over the building. By morning, only ten people on the roof had survived.

OVERPOWERED
Black with muck scoured from the harbor, the first tsunami wave carrying vans and boats pours over a seawall in Miyako, Japan, on March 11, 2011.

HOLDING ON
As waves battered the disaster-readiness center in Minamisanriku, 10 people, including Jin Sato, survived by clinging to handrails and a radio antenna.

Japan leads the world in earthquake and tsunami preparation. High seawalls shield many coastal towns, and well-marked tsunami evacuation routes lead to safety. Tsunami warnings are sent out to the population soon after an earthquake hits. Together these measures saved many lives; Miki Endo alone may have saved thousands. The Tohoku earthquake itself did much less damage than it would have in other countries, yet between 16,000 and 20,000 died because of the tsunami.

Sato had already survived a big tsunami in 1960, when a 14-foot wave washed through Minamisanriku. An 18-foot seawall was built after that. "We thought we would be safe," Sato says. "But this one was three times that height."

It's likely there will be many Minamisanrikus in the future. In 2004, the deadliest tsunami in history killed nearly 230,000 people in the Indian Ocean, where tsunami preparations are generally poor. A tsunami devastated the Pacific Northwest of the United States about 300 years ago, and geologists say another is inevitable.

KILLER WAVES

In the fifth century B.C. the Greek historian Thucydides was the first person to document the connection between tsunamis and earthquakes. "Without an earthquake I do not see how such things could happen," he wrote. Actually, they can. Landslides can cause local tsunamis, such as the one that surged 1,700 feet up a hillside in Lituya Bay, Alaska. All it takes is lots of rock moving abruptly in lots of water.

The vast majority of tsunamis, however, are caused by seafloor earthquakes along faults called subduction zones. Most are in the Pacific and Indian Oceans. Along those boundaries two of Earth's **tectonic plates** collide, and the one carrying dense oceanic crust slides under the less dense continental one. Normally this happens smoothly, a few inches a year. But sometimes the plates become stuck. After centuries the plates suddenly become unstuck, releasing huge amounts of energy. In the Tohoku earthquake, much of that energy went into raising and lowering the water, creating a tsunami. During a tsunami, all the water moves from the seafloor up. At first, it spreads out in low waves that may be hundreds of miles long. In deep water the waves are barely noticeable, but they grow to dangerous heights in shallower coastal waters.

The Indonesian tsunami on December 26, 2004, killed people all around the Indian Ocean. It began off the northwest coast of Sumatra with a thousand-mile-long rupture on the Sunda megathrust, a fault under the Indian Ocean. Indonesia, the closest country, suffered more than any other, with nearly 170,000 dead.

In the wake of that disaster several countries cooperated to expand the use of a tsunami-detecting system. The system consists of instruments anchored to the seafloor that measure pressure changes caused by passing tsunamis. When a device detects a change, it sends a signal to a surface buoy (BOO-ee), or a float that relays a warning to at-risk areas.

In 2004 only six of these buoys were in service, none in the Indian Ocean. Even if they had existed, many countries in the region had no national warning centers. Tragically, 16,000 people died in India, even though it took the tsunami two hours to arrive. There are now 53 detector buoys operating worldwide, including six in the Indian Ocean, so another tragedy like 2004 is less probable.

The Tohoku earthquake shocked most **seismologists**, who didn't think a quake that strong could happen in the Japan Trench. Yet the evidence was there. A research team from Tohoku University had discovered separate layers of sand deposited around their city by three giant tsunamis over the past 3,000 years. Because the last tsunami had struck more than 1,100 years earlier, the next one appeared to be overdue.

REGIONS AT RISK

"I think all subduction zones are guilty until proven otherwise," asserts Kerry Sieh. Sieh is a leading expert on ancient earthquakes and tsunamis. The historical record is too short, he says, because it ignores long-dormant faults that could generate killer tsunamis. Sieh pulls up a map on his computer of the Manila Trench, just west of the Philippines. "It's 800 miles long and hasn't done anything big in 500 years. If it broke in [a very strong quake], it would have very serious consequences along the Chinese coast."

Another danger area is the Cascadia subduction zone that runs off the coast from California to Canada. The most recent tsunami there happened in 1700. Based on data going back 10,000 years, the region seems to have one major earthquake about every 250 years. It's unclear how bad the next one will be.

A lot depends on the season, says Nathan Wood, a geographer with the U.S. Geological Survey. "The Pacific Northwest coast is sparsely populated for the most part, and many people are less than a mile from high ground," Wood says. "But in the summer there can be 100,000 people on the coast."

Sheltered by the Olympic Peninsula, Seattle, Washington, would be spared the worst of a Cascadia tsunami. But shallower cracks in the crust extend under Puget Sound, the bay that connects Seattle to the Pacific Ocean. A moderate tsunami launched near Seattle might be more damaging than a giant one from off the coast. It last happened about a thousand years ago.

The fault that most worries Sieh, though, is the Sunda megathrust. He had been studying it for a decade before the 2004 tsunami. The earthquake happened near the northern end of the fault. "That particular stretch, from northern Sumatra up to the Andaman Islands, was on nobody's radar screen," says Sieh.

He had been working several hundred miles to the south, studying the seismic history of west central Sumatra. His team put together a disturbing picture. For the past 700 years large earthquakes had occurred in pairs about every 200 years, with each pair separated by about 30 years. The last two happened in 1797 and 1833. The next pair was about due.

In July 2004 Sieh and his colleagues began distributing posters warning about tsunamis. Five months later northern Sumatra was devastated, and Sieh's group got a lot of publicity. "We got credit we didn't deserve," he says. "Our forecast was for a different part of the fault."

But that forecast still stands. In fact, says Sieh, the expected first of the latest pair of earthquakes happened in 2007. At Padang, the tsunami was only around three feet high. Padang is a low-lying city of more than 800,000 and the capital of West Sumatra. Sieh fears it may not be spared when the second one happens.

Sieh explains, "There's never been a more precise forecast of a giant earthquake, period." He continues. "Our forecast is for an 8.8 magnitude earthquake in the next 30 years. Nobody can say whether it will be 30 seconds from now or 30 months. But we can say it's very likely to happen within 30 years."

"What are you going to do?" Sieh adds. "Move the whole city for something that happens once every 200 years?"

To Sieh, that is the central problem for people facing the unlikely but dire event of a major tsunami. "The fundamental problem," he says, "is not that scientists don't know enough, and it's not that engineers don't engineer enough. The fundamental problem is that there are seven billion of us, and too many of us are living in places that are dangerous."

When the next tsunami hits Padang, most people will have no more than 20 minutes to run a mile to safety. The death toll will probably be much higher than Japan's in 2011—more like the 90,000 lost in Banda Aceh, Indonesia, in 2004.

DEVASTATION
In Banda Aceh, Indonesia, an elephant clears the debris from houses destroyed by the tsunami that struck the city in 2004.

AFTERMATH

Life in Banda Aceh these days blends the horrific with the miraculous. The tragedy that killed so many also brought peace, ending decades of war between rebels and the Indonesian government. Economic aid has helped rebuild the city, but everyone knows someone who died. "Sometimes when I close my eyes, I can still hear people screaming," one woman told me. In a small park children play near a 2,600-ton ship, dropped by the tsunami on top of several houses.

On a sultry morning in Padang, an elementary school is preparing for a disaster. Students practice protecting themselves from earthquake **debris** by holding their backpacks over their heads. Squatting in circles, they chant together. "It's to keep them calm during a real emergency," Patra Rina Dewl explains.

Patra heads a nonprofit tsunami-awareness organization called Kogami. She and her staff have started tsunami drills in schools. Because there is no high ground nearby, students are trained to run two miles inland. But some can't run fast enough. "The first graders take 40 minutes to reach the safe area," says Elivia Murni, one of the teachers. "They will disappear if the tsunami comes. We won't be able to save them."

There are about a thousand schools along the coast of West Sumatra, but Kogami can't help some of the fishing villages. "Sometimes I can't sleep at night," Patra says. "There are no escape routes for them here."

The morning after the tsunami in Minamisanriku, Jin Sato and the others on the roof were cold, wet, and exhausted. They climbed down fishing nets that had washed up against the building and found other survivors on a

STRANDED
A pleasure boat sits on top of a building in Otsuchi, Japan, deposited there by the March 11, 2011 tsunami.

nearby hill. Sato's office is now in a building on that hill. His hands are still scarred from gripping the radio antenna.

The town Sato grew up in is gone, but he is still responsible for many of its people, some living in temporary shelters. Minamisanriku may never be rebuilt, and that is a source of anxiety for the survivors. "People want to stay here, where their ancestors lived and died," says Sato. "They don't want to move."

THINK ABOUT IT! ||||||||||||||||||||||||||||||||

1 **Describe Geographic Information** Why are tsunamis barely noticeable in the middle of the ocean?

2 **Make Predictions** What is likely to happen the next time there is an earthquake at the Sunda megathrust? Support your answer with evidence from the article.

BACKGROUND & VOCABULARY

debris *n.* (duh-BREE) the pieces that remain of something that has been destroyed

fault *n.* the fracture along which the blocks of Earth's crust on either side have moved relative to one another

seismologist *n.* (syz-MAWL-uh-jist) a scientist who studies earthquakes

tectonic plate *n.* a piece of Earth's crust that lays over a layer of molten rock below

Time to Run

Adapted from "A Time to Run," by Marie Mutsuki Mockett, in *National Geographic*, February 2012

Marie Mutsuki Mockett is a novelist and nonfiction writer. Here, she shares her thoughts and memories about Japan, her mother, and tsunamis.

I recently found journals I kept as a child while traveling through Japan with my mother. They are written in Japanese in pencil, and each entry is accompanied by a picture drawn with colored pen. In one a girl (me) swims off a beach. In another a woman (my mother) carries an umbrella, while a child clings to her back. The mother is knee high in dark blue water as heavy, angry raindrops fill the sky. The day before, we had been to the Nebuta Matsuri, a festival in which huge lanterns in the shapes of gods and heroes wended through hot, dark summer streets. There was flooding the next day, and though my mother laughed as she carried me to safety, we feared what would happen if the rain didn't stop. In another picture I stand under gigantic, chandelier-like ornaments in the city of Sendai. The decorations are part of Sendai's **Tanabata** star festival, in which separated lovers, represented by the stars Vega and Altair, are reunited for just one night.

All these places are beach towns. When we visited, my mother always asked me the same thing. "What do you do if the water suddenly goes away?"

"Run," I would answer.

"Why?"

As I got older, I found this questioning annoying and thought my mother was overdramatic. Born in Japan, she had trained as an opera singer in Europe, where she met my father, an American. Both had a tendency to behave as though they were on a stage. Sometimes I got to be onstage with them and sometimes I was the audience. It was hard to know what to take seriously.

"Come on. Why?" she'd repeat.

"Because it means there is a tsunami."

Later, I would sometimes gaze at the ocean and try to imagine what it would look like all sucked away. How far would it recede, and how would it come back in? What exactly was a tsunami? No one I knew in Japan, including my mother, had ever seen one. Everyone was much more afraid of typhoons or earthquakes, even referring to Japan as "earthquake country."

My mother's warning and preparation came back to me when I awoke on March 11, 2011, to the horrendous news. Places in the **Tohoku** region that I had visited in childhood had been devastated by an earthquake and tsunami.

Thanks to hundreds of amateur Japanese photographers, we have a clear idea of what occurs when the water rushes back in. It's still difficult for me to visualize what the ocean looks like when it is sucked out.

Traveling in Japan months after the disaster, I have been struck by how survivors speak about their former friend the ocean. Many Tohoku residents make their living from the sea; they were shocked to see familiar waters transformed.

Newspapers are filled with stories of those who had 15 to 30 minutes to evacuate to high land, which seems like sufficient time. Then again,

EYES OF A CHILD
These pages from Marie Mutsuki Mockett's 1976 childhood journal depict Onahama Harbor, which was damaged by the 2011 tsunami. The tall building on the left is a lighthouse.

what of those who, like me, were schooled to run but became curious about the watery beast? Many survivors spoke of residents who returned to their homes after the first wave receded. One man went closer to the ocean to "watch" the tsunami after "missing it" the first time. His mother begged him not to, but he insisted, and she accompanied him. Both perished.

The world has praised the methodical, **stoic** nature of the Japanese for the way they cleaned up and cared for one another. But these qualities existed before the disaster. It is painful for a culture that prides itself on maintaining harmony, and on its Buddhist nature of compassion, to wonder what more could have been done to prevent 16,000 deaths. Ryoko Mita, who is married to my mother's cousin, lamented: "The tsunami revealed our *yudan* [carelessness] and our *ogori* [overconfidence]."

Centuries-old stones warning of past tsunamis dot the coastline of northeast Japan. But just as I was of two minds about my mother's warnings, it seems too easy to dismiss an urgent message from the past. Unlike earthquakes, which are commonplace in Japan, tsunamis often skip a generation, giving them an obscure and unpredictable power.

"Do you see the sea differently now?" I asked Rumi Sakuyama, a lifelong resident of Japan's northeast coast. "Such a peaceful ocean . . . to do such a thing," she replied, gazing out at the quiet water. "A tsunami like this will probably never happen again during my life." And therein lies the danger.

THINK ABOUT IT! |||||||||||||||||||||||||||||||

1 Compare and Contrast How did the author's attitude about tsunamis change after what she learned on March 11, 2011?

2 Find Main Ideas and Details What point does the author make about human nature in this article, and how does she support her conclusion?

BACKGROUND & VOCABULARY

stoic *adj.* (STOH-ihk) uncomplaining about bad luck or pain

Tanabata *n.* (tan-ah-BAH-tah) the name of a festival usually celebrated on the seventh day of the seventh lunar month of the Japanese calendar; literally, "Evening of the seventh"

Tohoku *n.* (toh-HOH-koo) the region occupying the northern end of Honshu, Japan's largest island

Document-Based Question

August, 2005: Just before landfall, Hurricane Katrina weakened from Category 5 to Category 3 and veered east, sparing New Orleans from its fiercest winds. But the levees, or earthen ridges, built to hold back nearby Lake Pontchartrain gave way, flooding much of the city with eight or more feet of dirty water. Some wondered if the tragedy could have been prevented. Others wondered if the city could survive it.

DOCUMENT 1 Secondary Source
A Civil Engineer's Study

After Katrina, engineers and government leaders confronted questions about why New Orleans had suffered so much damage. Lawrence H. Roth, Deputy Executive Director of the American Society of Civil Engineers at Auburn University, shared this analysis.

Much of the destruction from Hurricane Katrina was caused not by the storm itself, but by a series of . . . unfortunate choices and decisions, made over many years. There were two direct causes of the levee breaches. First, several levees with concrete floodwalls collapsed because of the way they were designed. Second, many levees and floodwalls were overtopped by water pouring over them, eroding their foundations.

The lessons learned from Katrina . . . should cause all civil engineers to bring about shifts in the way they approach projects that [affect] public health, safety, and welfare.

from "Abstract: The New Orleans Levees: The Worst Engineering Catastrophe in U.S. History," by Lawrence Roth, on eng.auburn.edu, February 9, 2011

CONSTRUCTED RESPONSE

1. In what way might civil engineers use the tragedy of Katrina to help improve the levees surrounding New Orleans?

DOCUMENT 2 Primary Source
New Orleans Eyewitness

In 2005, the Hurricane Digital Memory Bank was established ". . . to collect, preserve, and present the stories and digital record of Hurricanes Katrina and Rita." Since then, more than 25,000 items have been collected. One contributor described being a member of a high school marching band rehearsing for a parade to celebrate Mardi Gras post-Katrina.

Flooded out houses, devastated cars, dead trees and that rotten egg smell littered my daily route to school. I had been exposed to that death for so long that it had become commonplace and less impressive. That is, until that first [marching band] rehearsal.

There we were, 100 students strong, instruments in hand. . . . The notes fell on nothing but dead front lawns, broken glass, and those spray painted X marks on shutters and doors. But the music sounded so crisp, clean, moving, and passionate. As I marched those streets, I was overcome by a swelling sense of pride. This was my city, not covered by death, but swelling with new life, a spirit unbreakable.

from *Hurricane Digital Memory Bank*, by Anonymous, on hurricanearchive.org

CONSTRUCTED RESPONSE

2. How did rehearsing for a Mardi Gras parade help this New Orleans high schooler several months after Katrina hit?

How do
extreme wind and water
events impact human lives?

DOCUMENT 3 Primary Source
Aftermath of Hurricane Katrina

New Orleans has many poor neighborhoods that were hit hard by Katrina. Much of the city was underwater for weeks, and many houses were completely destroyed. Few residents had the means to rebuild. More than a year later, wreckage in some areas remained where the hurricane had left it.

CONSTRUCTED RESPONSE

3. What kinds of post-disaster challenges do you think faced residents of New Orleans neighborhoods like this one, shown in the photograph below?

After Katrina, residents of neighborhoods like this one were unable to even reach their homes for weeks.

PUT IT TOGETHER ||||||||||||||||||||||||||||||||||||||||||||||||||||||||||||||||||||||||||||

Review Think about your responses to the Constructed Response questions and what you have learned about extreme weather and disaster preparedness from this book.

Make a List Use a two-column chart to list different kinds of wind and water disasters along with the precautions that should be taken for each.

Write How do extreme wind and water events impact human lives? Write a paragraph that answers this question using evidence from the documents and the articles in this book.

INDEX

SKILLS